Living on the Edge

Arctic Frozen Reaches

WENDY PFEFFER

BENCHMARK BOOKS

MARSHALL CAVENDISH
NEW YORK

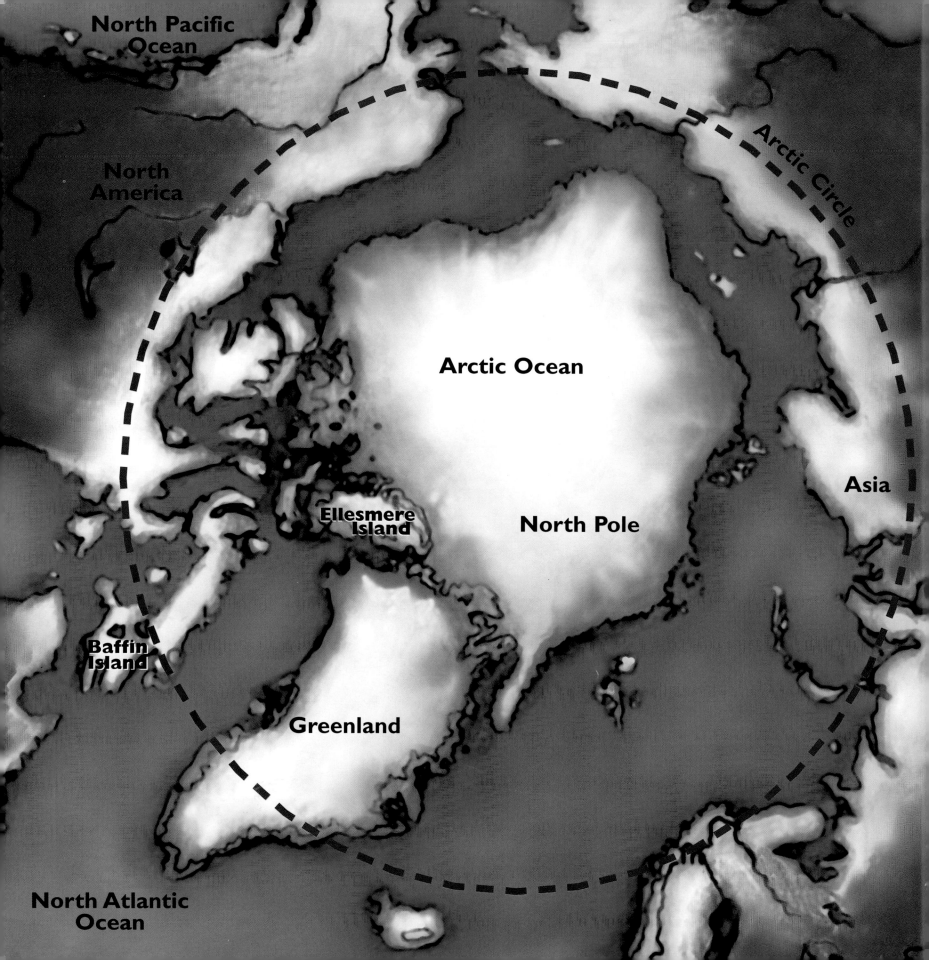

Contents

A female polar bear leads her cubs across frozen reaches.

Life on Frozen Land

In the Arctic on Ellesmere Island, winter brings total darkness, blinding blizzards, and bitter cold temperatures, sometimes reaching –70 degrees Fahrenheit (–57 degrees Celsius). That's much colder than your freezer. Only a few types of animals can survive. People adapt to the cold by putting on several layers of clothing, a hat, and gloves. But at seventy degrees below zero, how do Arctic animals stay warm?

Their shape helps them. Arctic animals have short ears and muzzles. Ears and noses that stick out get cold. When blood flows through long ears it cools the body. A desert jackrabbit has ears about 1 foot (30 centimeters) long, while an Arctic hare's ears are only a few inches long. Mammals and birds are warm-blooded. Their body temperature stays the same no matter what the temperature is around them. Cold-blooded

Arctic hares in the spring

5

An Arctic fox in its white winter coat

animals, such as frogs and reptiles, would freeze in the Arctic since their body temperature would be the same as the air.

Some Arctic animals hibernate to get through the harsh weather. Others have layers of fat, fur, and hair to lock in their body heat. Many have white fur coats that camouflage them from their enemies. Animals with thin or dark fur snuggle under the snow to keep warm. The snow traps their heat and the ground heat provides protection from fierce winds.

Sometimes Arctic animals need to stay on top of the snow. When an Arctic hare hops across the snow, its large hind feet act like snowshoes. In soft snow a hare spreads its toes out, too. Spikelike hairs under an Arctic fox's paws grip slippery ice and keep the fox from sinking in the snow.

Arctic birds and caribou enjoy the long, sunny summer days. But they migrate to warmer places for the dark, cold winter. Many other animals stay and endure winter's hardships. Keeping warm and staying on top of the snow are not the only challenges these animals face. They must also find food, raise families, and escape from predators.

Here are some of the hardy animals that live in the bitter-cold Arctic all winter and how they adapt in order to survive.

A musk ox with a dusting of snow

Polar Bears

Polar bears stay warm in the cold.

Polar bears survive the cold with the help of two coats, one of long hollow hair over another of short fur. Both coats cover a layer of skin and about 4 inches (10 centimeters) of fat. A polar bear's fat and fur keep its body heat from escaping. Its long white coat camouflages it by blending with ice on the Arctic Ocean and the snow on Ellesmere Island.

Thick hairy pads on the bottom of its feet protect its paws from the cold. And fur under its paws softens the sound of its footsteps. Like a cat stalking a mouse, the bear creeps silently over the ice then waits until a seal pokes its

A polar bear's long claws help it survive.

head through a hole in the ice. The polar bear uses its strong claws to pull the seal up through the hole. It does so with no more trouble than you have pulling a tissue from a box.

■ **Polar bears live here.**

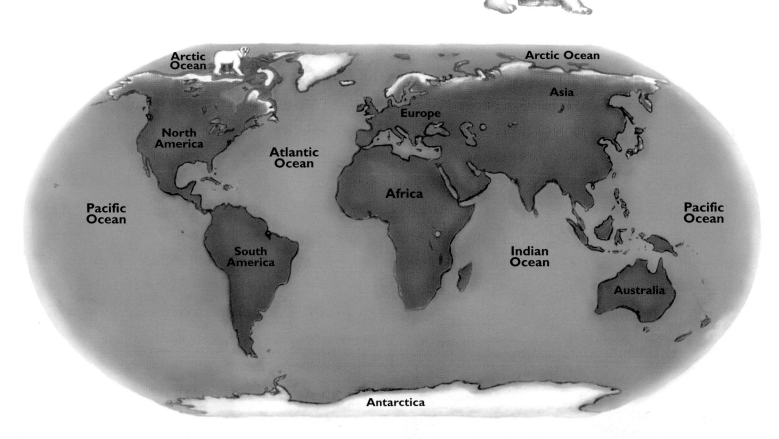

Polar bears have an amazing sense of smell. They can locate seal breathing holes under 3 feet (1 meter) of snow and smell a dead whale that is 20 miles (30 kilometers) away.

In late fall, the female bear chooses a snowdrift

A hungry polar bear

in which to dig her den. She uses her sharp claws to dig a tunnel, carve out a cave, then scrape an air hole in the roof, allowing stale air to escape. In her cozy den she gives birth, then cuddles her tiny, blind, toothless cubs to keep them warm.

A polar bear in her snowy den

A polar bear cub nursing

The cubs grow on their mother's rich milk, while she lives on stored-up fat. She needs rest to conserve energy, so she digs out a "play room" for the cubs. While she snoozes, they play-fight, wrestle, and bare their sharp teeth, learning to protect themselves.

Shaggy hair keeps a
musk ox warm.

Musk Oxen

These hardy animals have to protect themselves from 60-mile-per-hour (100-kilometer-per-hour) winds. The males face the wind and shield the rest of the herd like a furry fortress. Layers of fat under their skin and fur as warm as eight wool coats trap their body heat.

On top of the fur a shaggy mass of long black hair covers every part of the musk ox except its nostrils and lips. Musk oxen have the longest hair of any wild animal. One strand might be 3 feet (1 meter) long. Calves stand under their mothers' long hair, which hangs around them like a curtain. Sometimes herds huddle together or lie down in the snow to keep warm. They are so well insulated that even though their bodies are warm, they can lie on hard-packed snow without melting it.

Musk oxen travel in herds for protection. When wolves, their main predators, approach a herd, the musk oxen form a circle like a pioneer wagon train, shielding the young inside.

Musk oxen forming a protective circle

Musk oxen with their young

Shoulder to shoulder, heads and horns facing out, they stand their ground. If a wolf comes too close, a musk ox will charge and make quick jabs with its sharp curved horns.

Musk oxen get their name from an odorous musk gland under each eye. When ready to mate, male musk oxen rub that gland on their legs and the ground. The unpleasant smell warns other males to stay out of their territory.

Musk oxen conserve energy by wandering, feeding, then resting; wandering, feeding, then resting. In winter, sharp edges on their hooves cut through solid ice to reach twigs and grasses.

When the weather warms, musk oxen shed their long heavy coats, just as many people take off long winter underwear. In spring the young are born, wrapped in thick, dark, curly fur. They drink their mothers' milk and when only a few days old learn to nibble grasses and willows, a first lesson in survival.

A wolf howling

Arctic Wolves

As cold winds howl through Ellesmere Island's dark winter, Arctic wolves sleep outdoors. They curl in tight white balls with their bushy tails over their noses. The Arctic wolf has a layer of thick white fur to protect its body from the cold.

Wolves bond in family packs. When members of a pack go different ways, wolves often howl to keep in touch, to warn each other, or to let each other know where they are. An Arctic wolf's ears are so sensitive it can hear sounds 2 miles (3.2 kilometers) away. Its sense of smell is about one hundred times greater than yours. A wolf smells prey over 1 mile (1.6 kilometers) away.

A white wolf in winter

Wolves have long, strong legs and can leap swiftly over crags and crevices. Large pads and claws on their feet help wolves keep their footing on slippery rocks and ice. Wolves don't tire easily even while chasing quick-running Arctic hares.

Arctic wolves use clever hunting techniques. They dart at the musk oxen's protective circle again and again. This panics the musk oxen and breaks their circle. Then, the wolves rush inside, chase a calf away from the herd, and bring it

A wolf leaps onto an ice floe.

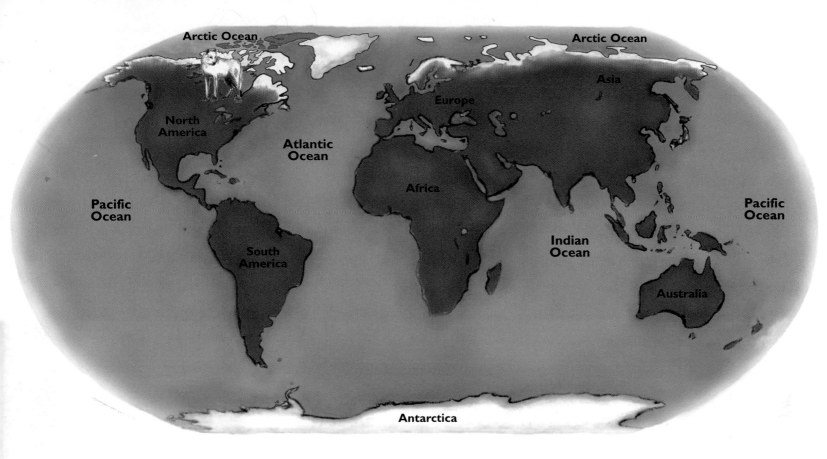

 **Arctic wolves live here.**

down. Wolves have jaws and teeth powerful enough to kill large prey and tear meat from its bones. An adult wolf can devour 20 pounds (9 kilograms) of food at a time.

After a long, cold, dark winter, when the sun reappears, a female wolf may choose a cave on a rocky ledge, crawl

A wolf pup has learned to howl.

inside, and give birth. Mother and pups will stay safe if the cave's opening is small enough to keep a hungry polar bear from squeezing through.

Other adult wolves in the pack hunt, eat more meat than they need, then go back to the den and regurgitate it for the pups. They bury leftover food in frozen ground to eat later during winter blizzards.

Snowy owls have bright yellow eyes.

Snowy Owls

In a blizzard a snowy owl will face the wind. This presses its feathers against its body to lock in warmth. Dense feathers make a waterproof and windproof coat. This feathery snowsuit protects it from harsh Arctic winds. And thick white feathers on its legs and feet protect them like warm slipper-socks.

Owls are predators. A snowy owl can see prey on the ground while flying as high as a small airplane. An owl's hearing is extraordinary. Its keen ears can detect lemmings under the snow.

When it hears soft footsteps it swoops down. With powerful legs and long curved talons, it plunges into the snow and snatches its prey. After the owl eats, its strong stomach juices dissolve the parts of the meal its body can use. Then it regurgitates pellets made of prey's bones, teeth, and fur.

Snowy owls use their talons to seize food.

A snowy owl flies to its nest.

Snowy owls are protective parents. To make a nest, the female scoops earth from the top of a hummock and then lays her eggs. She places feathers around the nest to protect her eggs. Her mate brings food and

A female snowy owl in her nest

An owlet, just hatched

Young snowy owls eat and grow and change.

guards the nest. Using his powerful legs and sharp talons he will spike any Arctic fox that threatens his family.

After the eggs hatch, the owlets snuggle near the brood patch, the warm spot on their mother's belly. They nibble at her bill and feathers

24

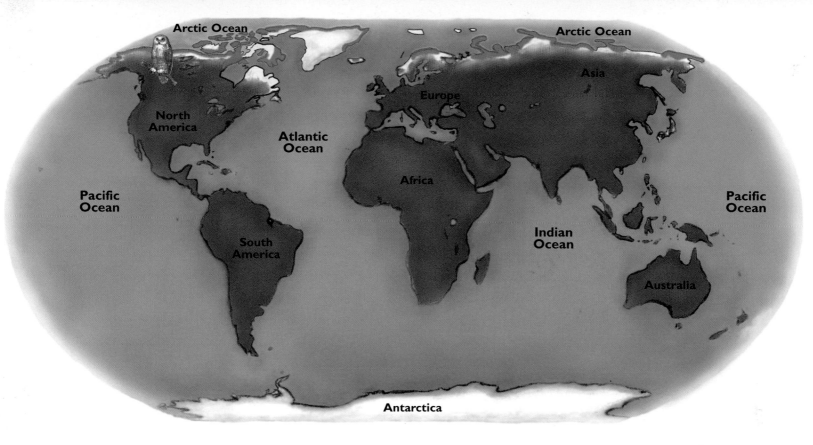

 **Snowy owls live here.**

to let her know they are hungry. The father tears mice, birds, and lemmings into small pieces for them. The young stay near the nest for about seven weeks. If an owlet strays, its father follows until it returns. When hungry birds circle above, the young owls gather together and sit perfectly still, looking like a pile of rocks.

Ptarmigans and Hares

A ptarmigan in her nest in summer

Camouflage protects ptarmigans (TAR-mi-guns) from predators, too. In winter their feathers blend with ice and snow. In spring their brown and yellow feathers look like spring grasses. A bit of white on their wing feathers blends with patches of snow not yet melted. In summer their brown feathers match their nest. In fall their gray feathers look like the earth. When they stay still they are almost invisible.

Ptarmigans depend on camouflage for protection since they don't have many other defense methods. Generally, they are timid birds, but if their young are threatened, they will attack.

A nest of ptarmigan eggs

A ptarmigan in spring

A flock of ptarmigans in winter

A ptarmigan in winter

Ptarmigan feathers grow denser in winter to provide more protection. Oily outer feathers keep ptarmigans dry. Feathers on their feet, called snowshoe feathers, help keep their feet warm. Even their nostrils are covered with feathers. Soft down next to their skin keeps ptarmigans warm as they sleep in the snow.

Like ptarmigans, Arctic hares change color with the seasons. A white coat protects them in winter. And in summer, as they scratch out twigs and willow roots, their grayish to brown coloring keeps them hidden. If an enemy appears they depend on speed to escape. They run fast, zigzagging around hummocks. If a predator

Arctic hares changing colors

A baby hare with flattened ears

An Artic hare on
Ellesmere Island

comes close they scatter, hide behind rocks, and lie still, flattening their ears against their bodies to keep from being seen.

When wolves chase them, hares hide among musk oxen for protection. Since musk oxen eat only plants, the hares don't fear them. But they must stay alert since they are food for so many other animals. They stand tall on their strong hind legs to view the landscape. Large eyes help them see far. And though their ears are not as large as some, Arctic hares can still hear well.

Even though its hair grows longer and thicker in winter, a hare needs to sit on the large pads on its hind feet to protect its body from the cold earth. Arctic hares cluster, then flatten their ears and huddle together for warmth. In winter they dig caves in snowdrifts and let blankets of snow protect them from the cold.

Arctic animals have adapted to the challenges of their brutal land in various ways. Having a compact body, warm blood, white fur, snowshoe feet, sharp hooves, snow-shovel claws, amazing senses, strong hunting skills, dense feathers, and protective parents helps. By adapting to their harsh environment many rugged animals survive and make this lonely, bitter-cold world their home.

Other Animals Adapt and Survive

Lemmings are thick-furred rodents that spend all winter under the snow. Without this snowy blanket they could die in the cold. Lemmings grow "snow shovels" in winter. Two middle claws on their forefeet become longer and larger. With these they can dig long snow tunnels to snuggle in and reach frozen grasses to nibble on. Lemmings build nests of dry grass deep inside the tunnels, lining them with feathers or musk ox wool. They stay warm enough to mate and raise their young.

A lemming in summer

Ground Squirrels survive the cold by hibernating seven months of the year. All summer they gather tundra plants, seeds, and fruits. They eat some and store more to eat when they wake up in the spring before new plants begin to grow. In fall they line their dens with lichens, leaves, and musk ox hair. Each den is an amazing maze of tunnels with many openings to slip into when danger looms. Always on the lookout,

An Arctic fox and a polar bear, together in a cold world

An Arctic ground squirrel feeding

ground squirrels sound a warning when they detect danger. A scolding sound means a predator, perhaps an Arctic wolf, is prowling nearby. A shrill whistle means a snowy owl or other bird of prey is circling overhead.

Weasels are good hunters with keen sight and smell. All winter they slip through dark snow tunnels trying to catch lemmings. Weasels sniff, pounce, bite, and then wrap their long bodies around their prey so it can't escape. Like so many Arctic animals, weasels turn snowy white in the winter.

Arctic Foxes, like wolves, rarely take shelter, even in freezing blizzards. Their heavy white coats keep them warm in winter. Their short

A weasel in winter

A white Arctic fox,
with a dusting of snow

ears, stubby legs, and small muzzles prevent the loss of body heat. And their thick, oily fur sheds water to keep the foxes dry. Arctic fox pups are born in the spring and summer. In years when lemmings are plentiful, each litter may have a dozen or more pups. Parents must kill about thirty-six lemmings each day for twelve pups. Before the young leave the den the parents must catch ten times as many. When the lemming population is small the female has fewer pups. Otherwise her family would starve.

GLOSSARY

ADAPT   adjust to one's surroundings

BROOD PATCH   a warm place on a bird's body where feathers have been shed

CAMOUFLAGE   coloring or body shape that makes an animal hard to see in its natural surroundings

COLD-BLOODED   having blood that becomes colder or warmer as the air or water temperature changes

HIBERNATE   to spend the winter in a kind of sleep

HOLLOW HAIR   hair that stays full of air to trap body heat

HUMMOCK   a low hill or a raised mound in a field of ice

INSULATE   to cover something with a material that keeps heat or sound from escaping

PREDATOR   an animal that hunts other animals for food

PREY   an animal hunted for food by another animal

REGURGITATE   to bring partly digested food from the stomach back to the mouth

TALON   a claw on a bird of prey

WARM-BLOODED   having a body temperature that stays the same no matter what the surrounding temperature is

FIND OUT MORE

Books

Bruemmer, Fred. *Arctic Animals: A Celebration of Survival.* Ashland, WI: NorthWord Press, 1986.

Gilbreath, Alice. *The Arctic and Antarctica: Roof and Floor of the World.* Minneapolis, MN: Dillon Press, 1988.

Kalman, Bobbie. *Arctic Animals.* New York: Crabtree Publishing Company, 1993.

Pfeffer, Wendy. *Arctic Wolves.* Parsippany, NJ: Silver Press, 1997.

———. *Polar Bears.* Parsippany, NJ: Silver Press, 1997.

———. *Snowy Owls.* Parsippany, NJ: Silver Press, 1997.

Web Sites

http://seaworld.org/arctic (Animals of the Arctic)

http://tqjunior.thinkquest.org/3500 (Wild Arctic Activities)

INDEX

Page numbers for illustrations are in boldface.

ABOUT THE AUTHOR

Wendy Pfeffer, an award-winning author of fiction and non-fiction books, enjoyed an early career as a first grade teacher. Now a full-time writer, she visits schools, where she makes presentations and conducts writing workshops. She lives in Pennington, New Jersey, with her husband, Tom.

For Diane, who encouraged me to keep writing

With thanks to Kate Nunn, who kept me on track

With thanks to Dr. Dan Wharton, director of the Central Park Wildlife Center, Wildlife Conservation Society, for his expert review of this manuscript

Benchmark Books
Marshall Cavendish
99 White Plains Road
Tarrytown, New York 10591-9001

www.marshallcavendish.com

Text copyright © 2003 Wendy Pfeffer

Maps by Sonia Chaghatzbanian
Maps copyright © 2003 Marshall Cavendish Corporation

Book design by Sonia Chaghatzbanian

Library of Congress Cataloging-in-Publication Data

Pfeffer, Wendy, 1929-
Arctic frozen reaches / by Wendy Pfeffer.
p. cm. — (Living on the edge)
Includes bibliographical references and index.
Summary: Provides information on how the various kinds of animals that live in the freezing-cold Arctic are able to survive.
ISBN 0-7614-1437-1
1. Zoology--Arctic regions—Juvenile literature. 2. Cold adaptation--Juvenile literature. [1. Zoology--Arctic regions.] I. Title. II. Living on the edge (New York, N.Y.)
QL105 .P524 2002
591.7586--dc21
2001007100

Photo Research by Candlepants, Inc.
Cover Photo: *Corbis*, Dan Guravich
The photographs in this book are used by permission and through the courtesy of; *Photo Researchers*: Jeff Lepore, title page, 12, 13; Dan Gurich, 4, 11, 28 (top); Brock May, 5, 30; Tom & Pat Leeson, 6; Mark Newman, 7; Art Wolf, 8; B & C Alexander, 10 (top), 29 (top); Stephan J. Krasemann, 10 (bottom); Alan & Sandy Carey, 17; M.J. Manuel, 22 (top); Karl & Steve Maslowski, 22 (bottom); Cordier / Jacana, 24 (bottom); Barry Griffiths, 26 (top); Kenneth W. Fink, 26 (bottom); George D. Lepp, 27; Charlie Ott, 28 (bottom); AH Rider, 29 (bottom); Tom McHugh, 32; Leonard Lee Rue III, 34 (top); Jacana, 34 (bottom). *Corbis*: Kennan Ward, 9, 24 (top), 33; Francesc Muntada, 21; Yogi, Inc., 23; George D. Lepp, 35; Richard Hamilton Smith, back cover. Accent Alaska: Hugh Rose, 14; *Robert Winslow*: 16; *Minden Pictures*: Jim Brandenburg, 18, 19.

Printed in Hong Kong

1 3 5 6 4 2